Confidence for Women

Simple Steps to be Confident and Attractive without Being a B*tch

By
Maria van Noord

© **Copyright 2018 - All rights reserved.**

The content contained within this book may not be reproduced, duplicated or transmitted without direct written permission from the author or the publisher.

Under no circumstances will any blame or legal responsibility be held against the publisher, or author, for any damages, reparation, or monetary loss due to the information contained within this book. Either directly or indirectly.

Legal Notice:

This book is copyright protected. This book is only for personal use. You cannot amend, distribute, sell, use, quote or paraphrase any part, or the content within this book, without the consent of the author or publisher.

Disclaimer Notice:

Please note the information contained within this document is for educational and entertainment purposes only. All effort has been executed to present accurate, up to date, and reliable, complete information. No warranties of any kind are declared or implied. Readers acknowledge that the author is not engaging in the rendering of legal, financial, medical or professional advice. The content within this book has been derived from various sources. Please consult a licensed professional before attempting any techniques outlined in this book.

By reading this document, the reader agrees that under no circumstances is the author responsible for any losses, direct or indirect, which are incurred as a result of the use of the information contained within this document, including, but not limited to, — errors, omissions, or inaccuracies.

Table of Contents

Chapter 1: Introduction - What is Confidence?   7

   Why Is Confidence Important?   8

   Signs of a Confident Woman   9

   Is Confidence Learned or Genetically Acquired?   11

   Being Confident Vs. Having Confidence   13

   Confidence and Self-Esteem   14

   Confidence and Assertiveness   15

   Chapter Summary   16

Chapter 2: Understanding Your Current Level of Confidence   17

   Self-Discovery with a Partner   23

   Chapter Summary   25

Chapter 3: How to Start Being Confident   27

   Growth Mindset   28

   Tips to Develop a Growth Mindset   30

   Learn and Practice New Skills   33

   Chapter Summary   35

Chapter 4: Self-Awareness - Define Your Core Values   37

   Characteristics of Core Values   39

   Self-Assessment Exercise to Identify or Define Your Core Values   41

Chapter Summary   45

Chapter 5: Setting Goals to Achieve Your Mission and Purpose   47

   Significance and Importance of Life Purpose and Goals   47

Self-Discovery Questions before You Set Goals	50
Daily Goals Worksheet for Women	51
Weekly Goals Worksheet for Women	52
Monthly Goals Worksheet for Women	53
Yearly Goals Worksheet for Women	53
Chapter Summary	**54**
Chapter 6: Tips and Tricks to Build Confidence - Part I	**55**
Affirmations for Confidence	55
Visualization Techniques for Confidence	58
Journal Writing for Confidence Building	61
Avoid Perfectionism	63
Chapter Summary	65
Chapter 7: Tips and Tricks to Build Confidence - Part II	**67**
Challenge Yourself Continuously	67
Love Yourself	69
Have a Positive Attitude	72
Chapter Summary	**74**
Conclusion	**75**

Chapter 1: Introduction - What is Confidence?

Confidence is a state of mind in which you feel capable of accomplishing a task or activity with little or no problems. Confidence is a reflection of your self-belief in your capabilities and abilities. Confidence is a trait that helps you take up challenging jobs. Confidence does not mean you will succeed at every task you take up, but that you are ready to accept failures too and learn from them.

Confidence is not a static measure. It is not something you will suddenly feel after one shopping spree. It is not something you get one day, and after that, it will remain with you for the rest of your life. You don't have to feel discouraged if you get up in the morning not feeling great about yourself.

Confidence is dynamic and changes depending on many factors including skill levels, self-awareness, ability to handle failures, and more. Building and improving your confidence is a lifelong process filled with ups and downs. Developing confidence is an evolving process that never stops right through your lifetime.

Jessica Williams, the tennis star, says, "Confidence is a journey, not a destination. Where Monday I'll feel shitty about my body, and on Tuesday I'll feel like the hottest bitch in the world, you know? I think it just ebbs and flows."

Confidence is rooted in:

- The feeling that you will get better at things when you put in the effort to learn and practice
- The feeling that you are capable of adapting to changes in the environment

Confidence comes from feeling good about and accepting yourself the way you are. You are happy with your strengths and humbly accept your weaknesses without feeling shameful or guilty.

Why Is Confidence Important?

There is nothing right or wrong about being confident or about lacking confidence. It is only a personality trait that comes with a host of benefits and is extremely useful for success and happiness. It is not a moral issue, and therefore, don't feel guilty if you think you lack confidence. In fact, many women lose confidence for multiple reasons such as:

- Receiving undue criticism
- Surrounded by negative people
- Negative self-talk in the form of, "I'm a loser," 'I'm stupid," etc.
- Negative body image in our endeavor to synchronize our image with the expectations of society
- Failing to achieve unreasonable goals set by others

Instead of feeling guilty for losing out on confidence, feel motivated to rebuild and develop it to leverage its multiple advantages which include:

You have an enhanced sense of self-worth – Your confidence will come from increased skills and knowledge and consequent success which, in turn, enhances your sense of self-worth.

You will be more joyful than before – Confidence brings with it some amount of success and an increased ability to learn from mistakes and move on. You will not feel like a loser anymore, thereby making you more joyful than before.

You will be free of self-doubt – When you are confident, it means you know and accept your strengths and weaknesses. This helps to eliminate self-doubt from your mind because you know what you can do and what you can't.

Signs of a Confident Woman

Oprah Winfrey says, "Think like a queen. A queen is not afraid to fail. Failure is another stepping stone to greatness."

You walk with your head and chin held high – Shoulders straight and head and chin held high are the unmistakable signs of a confident woman.

You have strong perspectives – As a confident woman, you will have strong and meaningful perspectives on various aspects of life including family, work, nature, and anything else. Confidence doesn't necessarily come with high levels of knowledge about that particular topic. It comes from your ability to perceive things your way.

You present yourself well in front of people – You dress well, you talk well, you interact with people nicely, and your overall presentation reeks of confidence.

You have a predetermined set of core values – You live your life on your terms which are based on a predetermined set of core values that guide you on your life path. You don't drift along but have a deep sense of purpose in life.

You give praise heartily – When you see someone doing a good job, you have no problem recognizing their talent and giving praise sincerely. Being confident ensures that you don't feel insecure with other people's skills thereby helping you give praise wholeheartedly.

You accept criticism in the right spirit – You understand and agree that you need to work on your weaknesses and the best way for self-improvement is to listen and act on constructive criticism. This knowledge allows you to take criticism in the right spirit. Hillary Clinton said, "If you want to be a change-maker, then you must learn to take criticism seriously, but not personally."

Is Confidence Learned or Genetically Acquired?

So, the question is, are womenx born confident or made confident? If you put ten babies between the 1-3 years together in a room, do you think their confidence level can be easily discernible? They will all behave more or less the same way, laughing at the same things and crying for the same reasons, right? However, put ten children who are over 10 years old in a room, and you will clearly begin to see how some are more confident than the others.

So, what happened between 3 and 10 years? People are influenced by the environment of their upbringing, their caregivers' attitudes, the various lessons they learned from their interactions with others, etc. We are all impacted by what we are taught and by whom we are taught these things. The impact of these lessons is felt on our confidence levels too. We learn how and what to think of ourselves, how to behave, and what kind of self-belief we should have based on our interactions with people and the environment. All of these elements affect confidence.

These elements become part of our lives during the early stages of development, and this aspect of our development plays an important role in our level of confidence. Therefore, it can be easily concluded that confidence is a learned skill and not a genetically acquired skill.

Yet, biology could play a small role in confidence. Some people could be born with a predisposition to being confident. However, such people's only advantage is that they will find it easier to learn lessons in confidence than those who appear not to be genetically predisposed to confidence. That's it. Nothing more.

Talent is an overrated item in the modern world. Hard work can never be replaced with talent. Speak to any of the achievers of the world, and they will tell you that talent without hard work has no value whereas hard work with a seeming lack of talent can take you to the pinnacles of success.

Thomas Hardy said, "The perfect woman is a hard-working woman, not a fine lady, not an idler; but one who uses her heart, hands, and head for her own good and that of the others."

Confidence is also closely connected to skill-building. The more you learn and the more you practice something, the better you become at it, and your confidence grows. Remember your first piano or music class? Can you recall how difficult the lesson seemed? You almost gave up after practicing for a while.

It is possible that your mother or father who believed in your capabilities urged you to keep trying, and you followed their advice. As you practiced a particular piece of music, you realized you got better at it, and your level of confidence to play it increased significantly. Therefore, confidence comes more from repeated practice and efforts rather than being acquired genetically.

Being Confident Vs. Having Confidence

The next question we tackle is "what is the difference between 'being confident' and 'having confidence?" 'Having confidence' is what you feel within you whereas 'being confident' is what others see of you.

For example, if you are giving a presentation to your colleagues, and you haven't prepared as well as you normally do, you might not have confidence in your present condition. However, your colleagues are already aware of your capabilities, and if you can 'be confident' in front of them, you just might pull off the presentation reasonably well backed by some amount of knowledge.

Another example of 'being confident' can be seen in some people who can put up a front of confidence despite knowing they don't 'have confidence' within themselves. They could use their gift of the gab to get away from tricky situations and appear confident in front of other people even though their skills are insufficient for real confidence.

Typically, women who 'have confidence' appear naturally confident in front of others. Those appear confident may not be able to keep the façade for long because the inner real self will soon reflect in outward behavior. So, it is important to have confidence by building skills so that you can be confident always.

Confidence and Self-Esteem

Confidence and self-esteem are related deeply, and yet are quite different from each other. Typically, self-esteem and confidence are directly proportional to each other. However, there are cases when they need not be aligned. For example, Emma Watson, the actress who played the role of Hermione Granger in the Harry Potter series and became a Hollywood star, oozed confidence in her role and won a lot of critical acclaim for her confident acting skills. However, she admitted to having self-esteem issues.

Self-esteem comes from a sense of self-worth. If your answer to the question, "Do I believe I am a worthy individual?" is yes, then your self-esteem is at a respectable level. But, if you are uncomfortable answering that question or are reeling in self-doubt, then you could be facing issues in that aspect.

Self-esteem is an identity issue and does not change across the different aspects of your life. If, for example, if you have a high level of self-esteem as a mother, then it is quite likely that you have the same high level of self-esteem in your office.

Confidence, on the other hand, can vary in different spheres of your life. You could be a confident mother but could lack confidence at your office and be uncertain of certain skills needed to grow and develop your career. Confidence is more an external trait that can be seen or felt by others whereas self-esteem is more an internal trait known only to you, and perhaps a few close friends.

Confidence in a particular skill can be built through the continued practice of that skill whereas the development of self-esteem is more difficult and requires you to change your overall perspective of yourself.

Confidence and Assertiveness

Confidence breeds assertiveness. But, the two are different too. Assertiveness must be necessarily showcased to the outside world whereas confidence does not have to be showcased. To be assertive, you have to talk and interact with people whereas confidence does not necessarily need to be expressed. You can feel confident about your skills and capabilities, but you don't have to show it to the outside world whereas assertiveness has to be expressed.

Chapter Summary

Confidence is knowing and accepting your strengths and weaknesses without being arrogant. Confidence is a personality trait that can be learned and mastered, and its multiple benefits can be leveraged to lead a more fulfilling and meaningful life than before. Confidence, self-esteem, and assertiveness are deeply connected and yet have many differences.

Chapter 2: Understanding Your Current Level of Confidence

Do you know your current level of confidence? It is important to know this so that you make informed choices about how to make positive changes in your life. This chapter is therefore dedicated to self-assessment quizzes and questionnaires which will help you gauge your present level of confidence so that you can make necessary alterations in the right direction.

Q1. When I am given a project report to do, I know where exactly I will find the required information.

1. Never 2. Sometimes 3. Very often 4. Always

Q2. Based on my lessons learned at college, I am confident I can do a great job in the workplace.

1. Never 2. Sometimes 3. Very often 4. Always

Q3. I like to take calculated risks.

1. Never 2. Sometimes 3. Very often 4. Always

Q4. I like to take up difficult challenges.

1. Never 2. Sometimes 3. Very often 4. Always

Q5. There are times when I may not know the answer to a question immediately. But I know where to find the required information.

1. Never   2. Sometimes   3. Very often   4. Always

Q6. I can confidently help my colleagues with any doubts in the workplace.

1. Never   2. Sometimes   3. Very often   4. Always

Q7. I confidently help my kids with their science and math homework even though I am not highly qualified.

1. Never   2. Sometimes   3. Very often   4. Always

Q8. Are you confident about appearing on a TV reality or quiz show?

1. Yes   2. I don't know   3. No

Q9. Would you give a big speech at your best friend's wedding about her?

1. Yes   2. I don't know   3. No

Q10. Do you think you are a positive individual?

1. Yes   2. I don't know   3. No

Q11. Do you let fear stop you from accepting risky ventures?

1. Never   2. Sometimes   3. Very often   4. Always

Q12. Have you ever disagreed with your seniors and bosses?

1. Never   2. Sometimes   3. Very often   4. Always

Q13. Would you contradict your boss or her boss if you believe you are doing the right thing and she is making the wrong choice?

1. Yes   2. I don't know   3. No

Q14. Do you believe that attack is the best form of defense?

1. Never   2. Sometimes   3. Very often   4. Always

Q15. Are you confident of crossing a busy highway?

1. Yes   2. I don't know, I have never tried   3. No

Q16. Would you take the ferry to an island even if you heard the weatherman say a storm was expected?

1. Yes   2. I don't know   3. No

Q17. Suppose you were asked to choose between two tasks by your boss. Would you take the more difficult one because you like to be challenged?

1. Never   2. Sometimes   3. Very often   4. Always

Q18. Do you believe you are more intelligent than the average worker in your office?

1. Yes   2. I don't know   3. No

Q19. Would you consider unraveling a woolen sweater with an intention to learn the stitches and then stitch it back?

1. Yes   2. I don't know   3. No

Q20. Are you impressed with orators and wish you could speak with such confidence too?

1. Yes   2. I don't know   3. No

Q21. Suppose you are alone at home with your kids as your husband is traveling. You hear a sound coming from the kitchen in the dead of night. Would you leave your bedroom to investigate?

1. Yes   2. I don't know; hope I don't have to face such as a situation   3. No

Q22. Do you do things that you don't really like just to keep others happy?

1. Never   2. Sometimes   3. Very often   4. Always

Q23. If your husband criticized you in front of your friends, would you raise your voice against such behavior?

1. Never   2. Sometimes   3. Very often   4. Always

Q24. Suppose you are invited to a party and that handsome hunk on whom you have a huge crush is also there. Would you walk up to him and let him know your feelings?

1. Never   2. Sometimes   3. Very often   4. Always

Q25. Do you feel happy about your talents and capabilities?

1. Never   2. Sometimes   3. Very often   4. Always

Q26. When you talk to people, do you confidently make eye contact with them, even if it is someone you are not particularly fond of?

1. Never   2. Sometimes   3. Very often   4. Always

Q27. When you have to say no to your children, do you look them in the eye and tell them no backed with valid reasons?

1. Never   2. Sometimes   3. Very often   4. Always

Q28. Suppose you went to a party, and someone misbehaved with your best friend, would you confidently tell the person to back off?

1. Never   2. Sometimes   3. Very often   4. Always

Q29. Are you happy your present levels of skills and knowledge?

1. Yes   2. I don't know   3. No

Q30. Do you need people to constantly praise you to feel good about yourself?

1. Never   2. Sometimes   3. Very often   4. Always

Q31. Do you get out of your comfort zone and try new things easily?

1. Never   2. Sometimes   3. Very often   4. Always

Q32. Are you excited about learning new things?

1. Never   2. Sometimes   3. Very often   4. Always

Q33. Do you forgive yourself for your mistakes?

1. Never   2. Sometimes   3. Very often   4. Always

Q34. Do you have your own set of core values and live by them?

1. Never   2. Sometimes   3. Very often   4. Always

Q35. Are you ready to bear the consequences of your actions and behaviors?

1. Never   2. Sometimes   3. Very often   4. Always

Q36. Are you happy with the way you manage your finances?

1. Never   2. Sometimes   3. Very often   4. Always

Q37. Do you balance your time and energy between your family and work, and also keep some free time for yourself?

1. Never   2. Sometimes   3. Very often   4. Always

Q38. Do you think you present a confident profile whether you are sitting, standing, or walking?

1. Never   2. Sometimes   3. Very often   4. Always

Q39. Do you choose your clothes with care and ensure you feel comfortable in them?

1. Never   2. Sometimes   3. Very often   4. Always

Q40. Do you usually feel positive and happy?

1. Never   2. Sometimes   3. Very often   4. Always

Self-Discovery with a Partner

Taking the help of a trusted partner is a great way to understand your current level of confidence. This exercise is a joint project that requires you to pair up with a good friend or even your life partner. First, think of an imaginary situation that requires you to be confident. For example, you could think of giving that speech at your best friend's wedding. Now, make detailed notes of the following elements basing your answers on that imagined situation:

Your emotions: will you be confident or nervous? Why?

_____

Friend's comments_____

What will you do about your emotions?

_____

Friend's comments_____

What will be your level of readiness? Would you have done a better job if you had time to prepare?

_____

Friend's comments_____

What if the audience was a smaller lot? Will your confidence level alter? How?

_____

Friend's comments_____

Answer honestly and after some thought. Your partner must do the same thing. She or he could have a different situation and a different set of questions too. Also, you can choose your own situation if the above situation does not suit your self-discovery process.

Next, give your notes to your friends, and let them read it and make their own comments in the 'friend's comments' place. Ask if they agree or disagree with your observations. Ask them to add comments that you could have missed out while answering the questions. You do the same for your friend.

This partnership will help you understand whether your outward appearance matches your internal feelings and emotions. If, for example, you had written that you would be nervous to give the speech, and your friend disagreed, then, perhaps, you are coming across as more confident than you are feeling. Think about these conflicting thoughts for a while and find out whether you are underestimating your capabilities or whether you are pretending to be confident even though you are nervous. Explore more self-awareness questions in such cases. For example:

Am I more skilled or less skilled than my outward profile?

Why do I see myself differently from how others see me?

In cases where your line of thought matches with that of your friends, then you get a fairly accurate idea of your current level of confidence.

Chapter Summary

The self-discovery activities in this chapter will help you gauge your current standing when it comes to confidence. Answer each question honestly to get accurate results using which you can plan your confidence-building path.

Chapter 3: How to Start Being Confident

What is the first step to making any positive change in your life? It is nothing but your decision to take the first step. Chloe Neill, in her highly popular book Midnight Marked, says, "They blew out a breath and did the thing all heroes must do—they took that terrifying first step." The first step of a new journey might appear terrifying, but, once it is taken all the following steps simply happen in real-time when you are totally immersed in the experience of the journey.

So, the journey to developing confidence starts with your decision to change today, and make all changes needed to build confidence every day from today. Start with the thought, "Today, I am confident, and I will endeavor to be confident every day."

Confidence building is not a one-time exercise. It is an ongoing process that requires you to be in a constant flux of learning and mastering new skills. Make a list of the skills you need to learn to increase confidence. Take one skill at a time and learn to practice it until you become a master. The most crucial element to be in a continuous state of learning is to have a growth mindset.

Growth Mindset

So, what is a growth mindset? Carol S. Dweck, a psychology professor, and researcher at Stanford is credited with the coining of two terms namely growth mindset and fixed mindset to discern between successful and unsuccessful people.

Unsuccessful people typically tend to have a fixed mindset in which they believe that their talents, intelligence, and capabilities are fixed and cannot undergo change no matter what you do. Driven by this belief, fixed mindset people don't attempt to achieve success. They just accept what comes their way and complain and whine.

Successful people, on the other hand, have a growth mindset which means they know that their present level of talents, intelligence, and capabilities are not fixed, and if they work hard and commit themselves to improve themselves, things can definitely change for the better.

Here are some differences between the growth and fixed mindsets:

• People with a fixed mindset tend to avoid taking up challenges, and this attitude blocks their path to success.

Growth mindset people, however, embrace challenges and treat them as opportunities for growth and learning. They are warriors who love a good fight irrespective of whether they fail or succeed.

- People with a fixed mindset either ignore or scorn criticism. They will not listen to any kind of criticism and avoid people who try to help them grow; another important reason for such people not to be able to develop their strengths.

Growth mindset people accept criticism in the right spirit and learn from it thereby growing with each new constructive feedback. In fact, people with a growth mindset are pleased to receive feedback and are thankful to people who take efforts. Learning from feedback is one of the primary reasons for the growth mindset for people to achieve success.

- Fixed mindset individuals believe that intelligence and talent are fixed. So, if their intelligence level is at one particular stage, then they believe it cannot move forward. As per the fixed mindset people, dumb people remain dumb, and clever people remain clever. 'Faults cannot be amended,' is what such people think. Here is what Confucius had to say about faults, "The only real fault is to have faults and not to amend them."

Growth mindset individuals have a strong belief in people's ability to build and develop their intelligence, talents, and skills through learning and practice. Such people are ever-ready to imbibe and learn new knowledge and skills.

- People with a fixed mindset don't try very hard and give up after the first or second, failed attempt. Such people refuse to learn from their failures.

Growth mindset individuals never give up and work hard to get better after every failure. They put the learning from their past failures to try again, and they persist until they achieve success. Margaret Thatcher said, "You may have to fight a battle more than once to win it."

• Fixed mindset people are envious of other people's success driven by their lack of self-belief and confidence.

Growth mindset individuals happily accept other people's achievements and success because such people know that if tried hard, they can achieve success too. Therefore, they don't grudge other people their success and happiness.

So, question yourself and see if you are a woman with a fixed mindset or growth mindset. If you are a victim of low confidence, then it is quite likely that you have a fixed mindset as it is a significant contributor to low confidence. The next step after making the decision to become confident is to develop a growth mindset.

Tips to Develop a Growth Mindset

Here are some tips you can put into practice straight away to develop a growth mindset:

Learn something new daily – Make it a point to pick up some new bit of knowledge daily. Listen to podcasts while commuting to work or read an article about a personal concern you have, or simply learn to sing one line from your favorite song.

Remember, learning is not getting it perfect the first time. Learning is only a way to tell your brain that new data is coming in and to be ready to imbibe and absorb it for future use. Knowledge is power in modern times. Never let a single day go by without learning something new.

Don't depend on anyone to learn anything. Today, information is at your fingertips, thanks to the ever-expanding world of the internet. Find online classes, read up articles, speak to people who are skilled about what you want to learn, and more. You can also engage with new people as often as you can to get new perspectives on life and its vagaries.

Surround yourself with positive-thinking people – Jim Rohn, the world-renowned motivational speaker and author of self-help books, says, "You are the average of the five people you surround yourself with."

So, if you want to build your growth mindset, surround yourself with people who have a growth mindset. People you interact with have a significant impact on your moods, behaviors, and way of life. Therefore, being with people who have a fixed mindset when you are looking to build your growth mindset will be counterproductive for success.

Challenge your fears – Fear can be so crippling that you can be frozen at the moment and you are unable to do or even think anything. Taking up any challenge calls for challenging your fears. The fears can be because of many reasons including fear of failure, fear of becoming unpopular, fear of being disliked, fear of losing love, and more.

Eleanor Roosevelt said, "You gain strength, courage, and confidence by every experience in which you really stop to look fear in the face. You are able to say to yourself, 'I lived through this horror. I can take the next thing that comes along.'"

It was her courage to face her fears that helped the former First Lady become a leader in her own right and participate and bring to fruition multiple benefits for the good of humanity in general and women in particular.

Never be afraid of making mistakes – Mistakes are not the end of the world. In fact, they are important for achieving success. Speak to any achiever of the world, and she will tell you that making mistakes helped in her learning and development far more than successes. Mistakes:

- Increase our desire to learn.
- Help us be more compassionate towards ourselves and towards others.
- Free us from debilitating fears and self-doubts empowering us to take increased risks.
- Reboot and rejuvenate our motivation levels which usually fade and get lost in the din of our daily grind.

When you try a new venture, be prepared that things will go wrong, and you will have to battle your external and internal demons to overcome the difficult times. But the efforts will be worthwhile because, at the end of an exercise, your confidence level will get a significant boost.

Learn and Practice New Skills

One of the primary reasons for low levels of confidence is the lack of sufficient skills. Identify the areas in which you lack skills, and work hard to learn and master these skills; a sure-shot way to build your confidence. Here are some tips on how to learn and master new skills:

Keep a curious attitude – Curiosity is a crucial element for enhancing knowledge and skill levels. If you have heard about a new thing in your office that you know will add value to your professional growth plans, then go home, and do plenty of research and learn more about that topic.

Ask why, what, how, when, and more such questions. Find answers to these questions and continue to garner information until your curiosity on the topic is completely satisfied. Don't take what one or two people or sources said to you for granted. Find information from multiple sources, and ensure you have different perspectives about the concerned subject.

The mastery of skill comes when you take a multipronged approach to learn it. When you become a master at something, people will flock to you for advice, answers, suggestions, etc. Consequently, your confidence gets a big boost.

Increase your versatility quotient – Try and skill yourself at many things. Learn to be good at your office work, learn to be a good cook, learn to be a great parent, learn some music, and read up and collect information about trending issues.

When you are skilled at many things, you can participate in any conversation with people of all ages, gender, race, and community. This wide-reaching attitude to involve yourself with multiple skills will help you be sure of yourself in many situations thereby building your confidence.

It is not necessary to be a master at everything. But it is essential that you know the basics of as many things as possible. This way you can participate in a group conversation, learn more from discussions, and help you to feel included and not excluded from the group.

Identify role models and mentors – Role models help you set a standard for yourself and give you a tangible goal of where you want to reach. Having role models make it easy to grow, learn, and develop your skills because you know where you want to reach.

While role models are people you want to copy, mentors are people who can help you achieve your dreams. Mentors don't hesitate to tell you when you are straying from your chosen path. They will not hesitate to give constructive criticism because they are your well-wishers.

Sometimes, role models and mentors can be the same person. For example, if you want to be like your mom, then she could be your mentor also, teaching and instructing you on your path. However, if you want to be like Michelle Obama, then you might have to find someone closer to you to be your mentor and well-wisher.

Chapter Summary

In this chapter, the benefits and importance of a growth mindset for building confidence were discussed. You also learned why and how you must work towards learning and practicing new skills to become a master at it.

Chapter 4: Self-Awareness - Define Your Core Values

Valuable people add value to your life. Your partner, children, friends, parents, boss, and others influence the way you think and behave. These people act as a guide in your life lighting up your chosen path, so you know you are taking the right direction to your dream destination. How are these people in your life a guiding light?

Let us take an example of your children. You value them a lot, and one of your life goals is to give them a sound education so that they grow up to be proud and responsible adults. So, you choose the neighborhood to live in based on the quality of schools in the given area. You will be willing to travel a long distance to your work as long as your children get to go to the best school. Therefore, many of your choices are based on the value and your priority of the various people in your life.

Like this, core values are the traits or qualities that guide you in your life path. They dictate your actions and behaviors. Suppose one of your core values is honesty. Then, when you are in a situation wherein you must make a choice between telling the truth and telling a lie, you will be guided by your core value to stick to the truth making it easy for you to make the right decisions.

Core values also called personal values not only make life worthy of living and uplift your morality but also form the driving force for your purposes and goals. Sheila Murray Bethel, one of the most influential business speakers today says, "You are the storyteller of your own life, and you can create your own legend, or not." So, it is up to you to create your personal values.

Core values define you, your personality, and what you stand for. They are life principles that you believe in deeply and are typically inherent in your psyche. You merely need to discover them. Core values become the guiding light of your life. When you don't know your core values, then it is tough to plan and live a life that you want.

Core values act as a compass to accurately show how to choose, live, operate, and behave to achieve your life purpose. They are your internal navigation system using which you process all your life choices and decisions. They become your standards for morality and competence. Core values are what you are ready to die for, and hope that you will be remembered for them when you are not on this earth anymore.

Recall an experience in your life that made you feel squeamish or deep down you knew that something was wrong. What were the emotions in your mind? Those negative feelings would invariably have been because your actions and behaviors were not aligned with your core values. Psychology experts opine that most often we feel excessive stress and anxiety when our actions and behaviors are incongruent with our inner values.

There are hundreds of core values available. However, most of us live our life aligned with the top 5-10. There are times when core values in your life could change and shift. You could unwittingly pick up core values from your family, religion, friends, school life, the outside world through print and social media, your role models, etc.

Core values are relatively unchangeable and remain the same for sustained periods of time. However, please know that it is perfectly okay to make changes to your core values by deleting those that don't make sense anymore or by adding those that have gained importance in your life.

Characteristics of Core Values

How do you define the core values of your life? What are the guiding principles of this exercise? Here are some attributes of core values that will help you arrive at your personal list.

• Core values should be practical to apply. You must not only know the techniques of how to use it but also know in what context to use it.

For example, suppose one of your core values is integrity. In an office scenario, when something goes wrong, then this core value should drive you to report the matter to the seniors. However, in a home scenario, if you are trying to get your toddler to eat something and want to use some form of filler (which could be the boogie-man, etc.), then this really does not come in the way of your core values, right?

- There should be a judgmental element in each of your core values which means it should carry your idea of what is wrong, right, or desirable.

Each person's core values form a unique set. They are like fingerprints of the concerned individual, and rarely, match perfectly with someone else's.

- Core values should be implementable irrespective of the physical state you are in. For example, you cannot really have physical fitness as a core value because it requires you to be in such a particular physical condition that allows you to implement this value. If you are sick and bedridden or stuck to one place for any reason whatsoever, physical fitness might not be implementable.

On the other hand, integrity or honesty can be implemented no matter in which condition you are in. You can display honesty even from your sickbed.

- Core values should be independent of external factors. For example, popularity cannot be a core value because you need the help of other people to like you to achieve this.

Self-Assessment Exercise to Identify or Define Your Core Values

How do you go about identifying which of the core values (from over 400) define you? Some of the core values include discipline, love, honesty, prudence, integrity, ambition, fun, health, friendship, respect, balance, family, and many, many more. For most of us, core values are typically inherent, and we unwittingly display them in our actions and behaviors. This exercise is only to help you discover these core values and label them appropriately to increase self-awareness. Here are some tips for that:

What were the five top successes and/or happy experiences in your life? – Give a name to each of these successful experiences and answer the questions given below for all of them:

Write in detail what happened in the event. When did it happen? How old were you? Who were the other people who were part of that experience? Write detailed descriptions.

_____

—

What emotions were ruling your mind and spirit in that successful or happy experience?

_____

—

What were your thoughts?

_____

—

What were the core values that were predominantly being played at that time? If the experience happened when you were very small, then it is highly likely you did not know the concept of core values then. However, now when you recall those beautiful memories, the predominant core values will come to you easily.

_____

—

What were the worst failures and/or unhappy experiences in your life? Take the top five – Write down answers for the same set of questions as for the happy experiences except the last one which will now be, "What were the core values you believed you suppressed during these events?" So, here is a template of the worksheet for the worst five experiences in your life:

Write in detail what happened in the event. When did it happen? How old were you? Who were the other people who were part of that experience? Write detailed descriptions.

_____

What emotions were ruling your mind and spirit in that unsuccessful or unhappy experience?

_____

What were your thoughts?

_____

What were the core values that were suppressed at that time?
_____

Next, identify your code of conduct – For this, you must ask yourself these questions:

- After my basic life needs including food, clothing, and shelter are taken care of, what are the elements that are essential to make my life meaningful?
- What are those elements of life without which I might survive but not be able to live a fulfilling life?

Here are some examples to help you understand what your code of conduct can be:

- Nature and its beauty
- Vitality and health
- Learning
- Adventure and excitement
- Creativity

Collect all the similar values together – From the answers to the above questions, you will get a list of core values that hold the top spot in your life. Now, the list is likely to be long and unwieldy. Combine and bunch together similar core values that mean the same thing. For example:

- Achievement, accomplishment, productivity, ambition, and other similar ones can be combined.
- Generosity, altruism, helpful, goodness, and other related values can also be kept together.

So, now your list will be easier to manage. Give one label to each bunch of similar core values. In the above two examples, the first set can be labeled as result-oriented, and the second can be called service-oriented. From this list of core values, choose the top few only.

It is important to keep your core values list between 5 and 10. If the list has less than 5 elements, then it is likely that all the important aspects of your life are not covered. If the list has more than 10 elements, then it will become difficult to track them.

The next thing to do is to rank your core values list. This might take more time than you think because ranking items that look equally important can be a challenging task. Here is a little tip. Revisit your good and bad experiences and see if you can identify the intensity of the emotions and thoughts that made up each of the experiences. The more the intensity, the higher its ranking.

After you have set up your core values list, and have ranked them in order of importance, make sticky notes of them and paste them in all visible places. This will help you to instill your core values repeatedly into your psyche making sure you can recall them whenever you have to make decisions in life.

Chapter Summary

This chapter taught you the importance of having a clearly defined set of core values with which you can lead your life more meaningfully than before. You also got a user-friendly template along with basic instructions (which you can tweak to your requirement) on how to identify and define your core values.

Chapter 5: Setting Goals to Achieve Your Mission and Purpose

So, you know your core values, and you have made sure they are deeply instilled in your mind. Now, you should use them to create life purposes and goals for yourself. Having purposes and goals helps you to lead a more fulfilling and meaningful life than before.

For many of us, finding our purpose can be quite a challenging activity. However, we must endeavor in that direction. Barbara Hall, the famous American novelist, television writer, singer-lyricist, says, "The path to our destination is not always a straight one. We go down the wrong road, we get lost, we turn back. Maybe it doesn't matter which road we embark on. Maybe what matters is that we embark."

Significance and Importance of Life Purpose and Goals

Winston Churchill said, "It's not enough to have lived. We should be determined to live for something." Having a life purpose that is divided into time-bound goals gives you multiple benefits. Here are some of them:

Purpose gives your life meaning and value – Unlike animals, human beings need to have meaning in our lives. We cannot simply eat, sleep, reproduce, die, and all the things that other living beings do, and find happiness and contentment. Our nature is primarily attuned to find purpose. A purposeless life is meaningless which, in turn, results in hopelessness and insignificance for you as an individual. A famous quote on life purpose goes like this, "A life purpose is the purpose of life."

Identifying and knowing your purpose simplifies your life – Your life purpose becomes your standard which helps you determine which activities are important and which are not. Discarding activities not aligned with your purpose clears all clutter resulting in making your life simple and lightweight.

You will not feel the burden of extra weight on yourself when you align your life path with your purpose. Additionally, decision-making is made simpler than before, and you will allocate time and energy appropriately without wasting them on unrelated and wasteful tasks.

Your purpose gives you focus and prevents you from straying from your chosen path – Having a predetermined purpose in life gives you focus. You know where you need to reach, and the goals you make for yourself to reach there will provide you with a clear pathway ensuring you keep your body, mind, and spirit focused on your purpose. In the absence of a clear purpose, your energies and resources will be scattered all over, and you will not be able to achieve anything. Also, having a purpose keeps you from straying. For example, if your purpose in your career is to become the head of your local office, then your path will consist of small steps leading to that final career goal. Every time you are tempted by an activity that is counterproductive to this final purpose, your mind will alert you, and prevent you from straying.

Your purpose prevents you from procrastinating – When you know you have to reach a particular goal within a certain time, your mind will raise the alarm every time you indulge in some procrastinating activity. Suppose you have a first date with that handsome hunk at 8pm at a restaurant near your home. Here's what you will do:

- Make sure you leave the office by 6 in the evening and catch the commute back home.
- Go straight to your wardrobe to decide what to wear.
- Then, quickly go to the bathroom, and take a shower.
- Change, spend some time wearing makeup, and looking good.
- You are ready by 7:30.
- You then walk or get a sibling to drop you off at the restaurant a little before 8.

While you were deeply engaged in these activities, it is highly likely that you had distractions such as social media and email notifications or a call from a close friend, etc. However, the goal of being at the restaurant by 8pm ensured you did not procrastinate and stayed away from all those distracting activities that took you away from your goal.

You may have done the entire exercise without even realizing how focused you were on your goal. That is how deeply-embedded goals keep you on track and prevent you from engaging in distracting procrastinations.

Therefore, it is imperative you find your life purpose, and then divide it into yearly, monthly, weekly, and daily goals so that you can keep track of them minutely and ensure you achieve your final purpose.

Self-Discovery Questions before You Set Goals

You must find your own purpose in life. No one can force you to accept a purpose. You must choose it of your own free will so that it helps you leverage all the benefits listed above. If someone else gave you your life purpose, then it cannot be called so. It only means you are leading someone else's life and not your own.

Venus Williams, the tennis superstar, says, "I don't focus on what or who I am up against, I only focus on my goals, and the rest takes care of itself."

Before you set down to write your purposes and goals in life, answer these self-reflective questions. You will find your goals hidden in your answers.

What do you enjoy doing the most in your workplace and at home?

What do you want more of?

What is your current status? For this, you should write down your current qualifications, your job description, your role at home, etc. You should also include how you achieved these things.

Where do you see yourself 5-10 years from now? For this, you should write goals you want to achieve (along with reasons) in your professional and personal life.

What are you going to do to achieve the goals you have set for yourself? Do you have to take any classes? Do you need help in any other form? How do you plan to seek help from the concerned people? Make detailed notes of your plans. This will be your 5- or 10-year plan depending on the time horizon of your life purpose. These plans will be converted and broken down into yearly, monthly, weekly, and daily goals.

How will you measure your progress? What are the metrics you will use?

Daily Goals Worksheet for Women

Before retiring to bed each night, complete this daily goal template. It could become your daily to-do list:

My goal for tomorrow is?

_____

What are the things I need to do to achieve my daily goal?

_____

Here are some classic examples for women that you should include in your daily goal list:

Go for my morning exercise or yoga (which could be part of your physical fitness purpose)

- Eat a healthy breakfast without fail.
- Meditate for 5 minutes before leaving for work.
- Complete the set tasks in the workplace.
- Spend some quality time with family.

Weekly Goals Worksheet for Women

Typically, goals for the week should be set on Sunday. However, if you want to keep Sunday totally free for yourself and your family, then make sure you complete this template by Saturday evening.

My goals for this week are:

_____

What are the things I need to do to achieve my weekly goal?

_____

Monthly Goals Worksheet for Women

My goals for this month are:
_____

What are the things I need to do to achieve my monthly goals?
_____

Yearly Goals Worksheet for Women

My goals for this year are: (your new year resolutions could come here; just ensure that these resolutions are aligned with your initial purpose).
_____

What are the things I need to do to achieve my yearly goals?
_____

Chapter Summary

This chapter contained ideas and insights into having purpose and goals in life. You read about the importance and benefits of goal-setting. The chapter also includes self-discovery questions which will help you arrive at your goals and daily, weekly, monthly, and yearly goal-setting templates for your use.

Chapter 6: Tips and Tricks to Build Confidence - Part I

What tips and suggestions are available to build confidence? This chapter and the next are dedicated to giving you valuable tips on how to build confidence.

Affirmations for Confidence

What are affirmations? Affirmations are positive statements that help in motivating and enhancing the positivity aura within and around you. Affirmations are short sentences that you repeat to yourself daily to help you achieve something or, sometimes, to simply make you feel better.

Louise Hay is one of the most influential proponents of positive affirmations. Each one of the chapters in her bestselling self-help book titled 'You can heal your life' begins with a positive affirmation. Affirmations empower you to work towards making your dreams a reality.

Benefits of Affirmations

•   Daily affirmations increase your ability to discern between positive and negative thoughts and facilitate the keeping out of negativity from your mind.

- When you repeat an affirmation daily and work towards your dreams, your actions and thoughts are synchronized with each other resulting in resonating effects of your efforts. Affirmations increase your levels of focus and motivation.
- Affirmations are aligned with the law of attraction. The more you affirm a positive thought to yourself, the more you will attract people and resources needed to make the thought a reality.
- Affirmations help you maintain a grateful attitude. Through affirmations, you can clearly observe the multitude of good things in your life for which you have to show gratitude. Your ability to sense even subtle elements that bring immense joy is increased through affirmations.
- Affirmations enhance your positivity which directly impacts your confidence.

Try any of these confidence-building affirmations. Repeat them to yourself as often as you can. Do try to make some of your own as well:

- I am mindful, calm, and confident.
- I am happy with how I am today even as I will continue to improve myself.
- I have faith in my abilities and strengths to overcome obstacles.
- I have compassion towards myself and others.
- I am strong, wise, and powerful.
- I am complete by myself.

- My most important best friend is myself.
- I am thankful for this gift of life, and I will endeavor to live it meaningfully and purposefully.
- I have learned a lot by facing challenges.
- I am a unique woman, and this uniqueness is my individuality.
- I believe each day I get better than the previous day.
- I deserve my dreams because I can achieve them through hard work.
- I am confident that I can complete all my responsibilities satisfactorily.
- I am a positive woman, and I always look for the best in any given situation.
- I enjoy receiving compliments because I know I deserve them.
- I feel grateful for my life and all its offerings.
- I do not hesitate to give praise when I see good work.
- I am always in a learning state, and I find valuable lessons in a worst-case scenario.
- I have talents and I work hard to bring them to the fore.
- I am an enthusiastic worker and learner.
- I treat my mistakes as learning opportunities and quickly move on.

Every time you feel your level of confidence ebbing, sit in your favorite spot ensuring you will be undisturbed for a little while. Close your eyes and choose an affirmation that is aligned with your current situation. Repeat it in your mind for about 5 minutes even as you try to focus on the positive aspects of your life.

Affirmations are not magical and cannot drive away your problems. But they compel your entire being to work harmoniously thereby enhancing your chances of finding innovative solutions to life's myriad problems.

Visualization Techniques for Confidence

Oprah Winfrey, one of the most influential women of today, and one who has, perhaps, experienced and overcome all kinds of problems available in the world, says, "You really can change your reality based on the way you think."

Visualization can easily be referred to as 'daydreaming' but with a strong sense of purpose. Visualization helps to crystallize your visions and dreams. The famous beach volleyball duo, Kerri Walsh and Misty May-Treanor, use a lot of visualizations to achieve success. In their minds, they take in the smells, sounds, and cheers of victory even before getting down to the court to start their match. Arnold Schwarzenegger dreamed of having a body just like his role model, Reg Park. Jim Carrey visualized holding a cheque of 10 million dollars.

How does visualization work? Here's how. Suppose you imagine yourself alone and lonely with no one to love you and care for you. What happens to your body? Automatically, your body shrivels up, and your shoulders droop in sadness, right? In fact, if you think very deeply of sad situations, tears well up in your eyes unwittingly.

Similarly, think of a joyful situation. It could be a fun picnic day with your family where your children are frolicking on the beach and playing around in the water. You can hear their laughter and chatter in your mind. Automatically, your face lights up, and you can feel yourself smiling. These are direct experiences that nearly all of us have undergone.

Multiple research studies have revealed a strange phenomenon. It appears that when we imagine something in our head, then the brain cells in certain primal parts behave as if the imagined scene is actually taking place. Visualizations in our head are believed to impact the working of our central nervous system and drive our body to do what we are imagining to make it a reality.

Benefits of visualization - Here are some excellent benefits of visualization techniques:

- It compels your subconscious and unconscious minds to delve deep and find innovative solutions to achieve your dreams.
- It helps your brain to identify and attract people and resources needed to achieve your dreams.
- Continued practice of visualization techniques activates the law of attraction in your life bringing mentors, role models, necessary resources, and other things required to realize your dreams.

- It enhances your levels of confidence and motivation.

Here is a visualization template that you can use for any of your dreams.

Visualization exercise: Suppose you had to say no to your sister-in-law the next time she asks you to babysit her child while she is out partying with her friends. First, prepare what you will be saying to her. Make sure you have learned your prepared speech by rote. Next, sit comfortably in a quiet place, and visualize the following events:

- Imagine yourself giving that prepared speech confidently to your sister-in-law
- Imagine yourself speaking in a strong tone of voice firmly and confidently
- Imagine finding counterarguments for each of her arguments
- Visualize yourself confidently say, "No, I cannot help you this time."

Journal Writing for Confidence Building

William Wordsworth said this of journal writing, "Fill your paper with the breathings of your heart." There are multiple benefits related to confidence-building when you start and maintain a journal. Some of these benefits include:

- You have clarity on your goals and your progress which drives confidence; you see the daily, weekly, monthly progress of your goals, and feel confident about achieving the final goal; you can also make changes to your goals whenever needed
- Journaling helps in recovering from the effects of negative emotions
- Journaling shows you the inconsistencies in your life helping you get rid of them
- Journaling improves your learning as you make notes of your daily experiences
- Journaling facilitates an attitude of gratitude.

You can also use journaling to convert your negative thoughts into positive ones. Here are some examples:

Negative thought: 'This is impossible to do.' To counter this negative thought, write detailed answers to the following questions:

- What are some of your biggest achievements to date?

•   Can you think of a similar situation in your life when you thought it was impossible, and yet, you finished it successfully?

•   What is the bravest thing you have done as of today?

Negative thought: 'I don't have enough knowledge and skills.' Answer the following questions with a lot of detail to counter this negative thought:

•   What are the topics you are excellent in? What areas do you excel so much in that others come to you for help? What are the training programs and certifications you have attended?

•   What are the things you can do to improve upon your present level of knowledge and skills?

Negative thought: 'I look so ugly and fat. I hate my body.' Answer the following questions to prevent being overwhelmed by this negative thought:

•   What are the best parts of your body? What are the elements for which you have received compliments from others?

•   What are the things you should feel grateful for when it comes to your body? A pair of strong legs for dancing, skipping, and walking? A pair of strong arms to do your daily work without having to depend on someone else? A beautiful smile that lights up your face, and those of your children?

Negative thought: 'I have insufficient good qualities.' Your answers to the following questions will help you counter this negative thought, and drive it out of your system:

- What are the things you possess that you should be grateful for?
- What are the top two compliments you receive from people?
- What does your loving family think of you?
- What are the things you have earned on your own that you are proud of?

Negative thought: 'I am sure to fail, so why should I even try?' Answer the following to counter this:

- What are the great things that will happen if you DID NOT fail?
- What will be the worst scenario? What are the ways you can manage yourself and the situation even if this worst scenario were to take place?

Avoid Perfectionism

Obsession with perfectionism is a bane and not a boon. When you are obsessed with perfectionism, you feel demoralized and exhausting. When you strive for excellence, then you feel motivated. Remember that no one is perfect. That is why even pencils have erasers.

Giving your best efforts to all your endeavors is a healthy attitude. However, the obsession to get every teeny-weeny aspect of your activity perfect is dangerous and unhealthy. Perfectionists are plagued by self-doubt which, in turn, prevents them from trying a failed venture again. Thoughts of obsessed perfectionists go something like this:

- I hate myself the way I am; I wish I was better.
- I am not satisfied with how this has turned out even if my team and I have worked long, untiring hours on it.
- The world is black and white; things are either right or wrong
- If I become perfect, then I will be content and happy
- I am not achieving enough
- Efforts have no value if the results are less than perfect

Obsessed perfectionists face a lot of unnecessary challenges and waste their time and energy. Perfectionists, invariably, are lonely and unhappy

They are always anxious and tired – In their efforts to achieve perfection, they use up a lot of energy on small things that have little or no value. Therefore, perfectionists are always tired and anxious

They have unhappy relationships – They want only the best for themselves, and there are no best partners in the world. Therefore, all relationships of perfectionists are unhappy and unfulfilled. Whether it comes to spouses, parents, children or friends, perfectionists never seem to find fulfillment.

Here are some tips to overcome the obsession for perfection:

Know and accept that perfectionism is not absolute – What is perfect for you could be only a 'good enough' for someone, and what is 'good enough' for you could be 'perfect'

for a different person. There is nothing like absolute perfectionism. The acceptance of this knowledge will prevent you from running after illusions.

Good enough is good too – 'Good enough' does not mean you don't try your best. It only means to let go and move on after you have given your best.

Know and acknowledge the imperfection in human beings – Humans are imperfect by nature. Our imperfections make us unique. Your fault is complemented by your spouse's fault thereby making your relationship workable.

For example, if you are a disciplinarian and your spouse is an easy-going person, then your children will have a normal childhood balanced beautifully by your discipline (when a situation calls for it) and his easygoing nature (when another kind of situation calls for it). If both of you were disciplinarians, your children's lives would be hell. Alternately, if both of you were easygoing, your children would never learn the value of discipline.

Most importantly, people who love and care for you will never reject you for not being perfect. Therefore, avoid perfectionism. Instead, focus on using your energies on building skills and your confidence levels.

Chapter Summary

This chapter discussed four different ways of building confidence including the use of affirmations, the use of visualization techniques, avoidance of perfectionism, and journal writing.

Chapter 7: Tips and Tricks to Build Confidence - Part II

Challenge Yourself Continuously

Challenging yourself, doing unfamiliar activities, accomplishing new tasks and projects, deliberately choosing a tough project, taking tough decisions, getting mentally and physically uncomfortable, and other similar kinds of activities are excellent ways of learning new things and building confidence. Also, helping others is a great confidence-booster. You must, of course, remember to equip and help yourself before you help others.

Every time you begin to feel comfortable in any place, you have lost the ability to learn anything new there. Challenge yourself continuously for learning and development. Whether it is at home or workplace, if you don't feel challenged by the work you do, then your confidence is stagnating. And stagnating is the beginning of a downfall.

Martin Luther King, Jr. said, 'The ultimate measure of a person is best gauged when he or she is passing through challenging and difficult times." Therefore, be conscious about feeling challenged and avoid remaining in your comfort zone for long. Your level of complacency is directly proportional to the duration of your stay in comfort zones. Expand your skills in multiple domains because mastery over new skills can build your confidence significantly.

Raise your standards to get better at what you do. Here are some great tips to challenge yourself continuously:

Indulge in activities that you hate – If you hate to cook, make sure you cook at least three times a week. Don't worry excessively about how the food turns out. The challenge is in doing something you hate for a sustained period of time. If you don't like a particular colleague very much, seek her out, and start a conversation.

If you are uncomfortable dancing, join a class and learn dancing. Doing something you don't like is a fabulous way to remain challenged and out of your comfort zone. Your body and mind will resist your efforts, and you will need all your willpower to fight them; a great way to boost your confidence.

Live with your biggest fear or hate for a week – For example, if you hate traveling by public transport, use it for a week. If you hate to give speeches, make sure you give presentations in your office whenever there is an opportunity. If you don't like your mother-in-law, invite her to stay with you for a week.

You are likely to be benefited in two ways from this exercise: one is you will be challenging yourself throughout the week, and two is that it is very likely you will see how unfounded your fears and hate were. Both of these lessons are useful for boosting confidence.

Stay away from what you love the most for a week – If you love your daily dose of Netflix or other video streaming service, then uninstall the relevant app(s) for a week. If you enjoy being on social media, stay offline for a week. Again, there are two benefits possible. One is, of course, being challenged, and two is you could be able to get rid of a bad habit that was eating into your productivity.

Do things differently - Brush your teeth and eat your meals with your non-dominant hand. If you are a very talkative person, consciously refrain from talking. If you are a very silent person, then make an effort to talk more.

The intention of these tips is to move you out of your comfort zone and challenge yourself. When you feel uncomfortable, your body and mind are very alert which is a great setting to learn new things and build your confidence.

Love Yourself

If you don't love yourself, no one will be able to love you. Your relationship with yourself is the first step to building relationships with other people. Kim McMillen, the celebrated author of 'When I Loved Myself Enough,' said, "When I loved myself enough, I began leaving whatever wasn't healthy. This meant people, jobs, my own beliefs, and habits – anything that kept me small. My judgment called it disloyal. Now I see it as self-loving."

Loving yourself does not call for selfishness or hating others or being narcissistic. On the contrary, loving yourself teaches you to be compassionate towards others too. Loving yourself only means that you are happy the way you are with all your strengths and weaknesses. Loving yourself only means you don't need external factors or people to make you feel complete and loved. Here are some fabulous benefits of self-love:

- When we love ourselves, we are okay with who we are, and our desire to be someone else disappears which, in turn, frees us from greed, resentment, and anger.
- We are free from anxiety about others' perceptions of us. We don't need to put up a façade anymore. Our life, behaviors, and actions are all authentic and aligned with our inner real self.
- We don't feel lonely when we are alone because we love our own company.
- We don't need to depend on anyone to manage our weaknesses because we know we will always be there for ourselves.
- We become responsible for our happiness and take action towards achieving our goals without waiting for anyone else to help us.

Some great tips for self-love:

Be grateful for the good things in your life – When you are grateful for the good things in your life, you feel happy to have them. This happiness makes you love your life and yourself, leaving behind resentment for what you don't seem to have. Gratitude is the first step toward self-love.

Build a community of people who love you – Yes, external people may seem irrelevant while discussing self-love. Yet, people who love you and care for you increase your self-love. Build a community of such people around yourself.

Maintain a clutter-free and clean lifestyle – Eliminate all kinds of emotional, mental, and physical clutter from your life. Maintain a minimalistic, clean, and clutter-free lifestyle that is free from all kinds of negativity. This kind of clutter-free lifestyle will give you a great sense of freedom and lightness that makes you see yourself in a joyful and happy perspective thereby increasing self-love.

Stay away from negative people – Avoid all the people who demoralize and weaken you and make you feel unworthy. Such people's attitudes drive you to think of yourself as a useless person who doesn't deserve love. This attitude is counterproductive to increasing self-love. Therefore, stay away from negative-thinking people.

Have a Positive Attitude

Frances Hodgson Burnett, the British writer of three of the most famous and well-loved children's books (Little Lord Fauntleroy, The Secret Garden, and A Little Princess), said, "If you look the right way, you can see that the whole world is a garden."

Keeping a positive attitude attracts positive elements into your life. And the more positive elements in your life, the more your confidence will grow. Here are some amazing benefits to keeping a positive attitude:

High levels of motivation – A positive attitude keeps your mood levels on a positive note which means you feel motivated to work hard and give your best.

Challenges are seen as opportunities – Every obstacle and every challenge is seen as an opportunity to learn and grow. With a positive attitude, you will notice hidden opportunities even in your bleakest moment because you are filled with hope and motivation.

Reduced stress levels – Negativity and negative thoughts use up your energy resources for unproductive work such as managing stress and anxiety. A positive attitude allows you to focus on the good things in all elements thereby keeping anxiety at bay. Your energy resources are then freed up to be used for increased productivity and efficiency which, in turn, reduces stress levels again.

Here are some excellent tips to develop a positive attitude:

Live mindfully – Living mindfully requires you to be immersed in the present moment. When your entire being is fully engaged in experiencing the present moment, your body and mind are not riddled with past regrets or future worries. A life of mindfulness, therefore, keeps you 'in the moment' helping you to live life with fulfillment and a positive attitude.

Describe your life and yourself positively – Words have a powerful influence on our minds. If you choose to describe yourself as 'average,' 'boring,' 'uninteresting,' etc., your personality will reflect these emotions. Contrarily, when you describe yourself as a fun-loving, happy, and joyful woman, then the impact of these words get passed into your personality, and you will feel the happiness.

In the same way, use positive words to describe the work you do. If needed, sit down and make notes with the right choice of words to use when you are speaking to people about yourself, your job, or your life.

Be conscious of every action you take and every word you say and ensure they exude positivity. Think before you do or say anything so that you get time to choose positive over negative. Surround yourself with confident individuals so that you can learn from such people and imbibe their positive qualities.

Chapter Summary

In this chapter, you learned more ideas on how to build confidence including challenging yourself continuously, loving yourself, and having a positive attitude.

Conclusion

The main takeaways to build confidence include:
- Your decision to start being confident from today, and then every day
- Building your core values and imbibing them deeply into your psyche
- Using the core values to develop your life purpose and goals; breaking down the goals into daily, weekly, and monthly goals to keep track of them
- Building self-awareness to know your strengths and weaknesses
- Building confidence through various methods including loving yourself, maintaining a positive attitude, leveraging the power of affirmations and visualization techniques, and many more tips
- Living life on your terms by knowing your limits so that you are not negatively impacted by what others think of you

Increased confidence brings high levels of self-esteem and assertiveness into your life helping you to lead a more fulfilling and meaningful life than before. For more detailed information about self-esteem and assertiveness, refer to the following books:
- Self-Esteem for Women
- Assertiveness for Women